Read Me

- All information supplied in
  purpose only and users bear the responsibility for using it.

- Although we took tremendous effort to ensure that all
  information provided in this guide are correct, we will
  welcome your suggestions if you find out that any
  information provided in this guide is inadequate or you find a
  better way of doing some of the actions mentioned in this
  guide. All correspondence should be sent to
  pharmibrahimguides@gmail.com

About This Guide

Finally, a straightforward and succinct microwave cookbook for newbies, seniors, students, instructors and homemakers is here.

This cookbook contains 50-day microwave meal plan that will introduce you to different varieties of food you can make with your microwave. And guess what? Many of these recipes are simple to make and are healthy.

PS: Please make sure you don't give the gift of a microwave without given this companion guide alongside with it. This guide makes your gift a complete one.

Table of Contents

General Suggestions for the Completion of the 50-Day Microwave Meal Plan

- Ensure you thoroughly read the manual that came with your microwave before you start trying the recipes contained in this book. Recipes in this book assume that you know how to properly operate your microwave.
- To allow uniform cooking, arrange food uniformly in a microwavable container. In addition, make sure you stir the food midway through the microwaving time whenever possible.
- Unless otherwise stated in a recipe, make sure you cover the food when microwaving. However, please make sure to vent the lid whenever possible so as to allow steam to escape. Alternatively, you may loosen the lid to avoid too much pressure from building up.
- You don't need to follow the 50-day recipes sequentially. There is nothing wrong if you cook the recipe for Day 15 after cooking the recipe for day 1.
- Please feel free to change the ingredients mentioned in the recipes if you think you know of better ingredients.

Day 1: All Vegan Blueberry Muffin in a Mug

So you want a special treat for yourself?

Then grab a mug-full of a blueberry muffin to make your mornings joyous.

What do we mean by *mug-full*?

Well, if you have a microwave then you can literally make mug filled muffins in a matter of 90 seconds. It is a pretty simple remedy to satisfy your sweet tooth!

Ingredients: (Serves 1)

- 4 tablespoons of self-rising flour
- 4 tablespoons of caster sugar
- 2 tablespoons of cocoa powder (optional)
- 1 flax egg
- ¼ cup of almond milk
- A handful of blueberries

Directions:

1. Mix all the ingredients (except the blueberries) in a microwave-friendly mug.
2. Keep on stirring until the mixture turns smooth.
3. Sprinkle in the blueberries.
4. Place it in the microwave for 2 minutes at high heat. If you cover the mug, make sure you vent the lid.
5. Let it cool for a few minutes before eating.

Once cooled. Devour this delicious muffin in a single serving!

Day 2: Cheap Thrills: Microwave Risotto

Would you like to cook risotto with little to no stirring? Here's a simple recipe that cooks by itself in the microwave and gives the same creamy and rich flavor.

Ingredients: *(Serves 4)*

- 3 tbsp butter
- 1 onion, chopped
- 1 clove garlic, minced
- 1 ½ cups vegetable broth
- ¾ cup apple juice
- 1 cup uncooked Arborio rice
- ¼ cup parmesan cheese, grated

Directions

1. Add butter, onion, and garlic to a casserole dish.
2. Cook in the microwave on high power for about 3 minutes.
3. Put the vegetable broth in a microwave-safe dish.
4. Heat the broth in the microwave for about 2 minutes or until it is hot but not boiling.
5. Add the broth and rice to the casserole dish and stir with the mixture.
6. Cover the casserole dish with a lid and cook on high for about 6 minutes.
7. Add apple juice to the rice and cook for another 10 minutes (or until done). Make sure all the liquid has boiled off.
8. Add cheese to the rice and serve. Enjoy!

Day 3: 15 and Under Chicken Couscous

A wholesome chicken couscous meal is what you need to satisfy your stomach and the taste buds at the same time! This recipe takes no more than 15 minutes to prepare,

Ingredients *(Serves 8)*

- 1 ¼ cups low-sodium, fat-free chicken broth
- 3 cups cooked chicken, chopped
- 1 packet toasted pine nut couscous mix
- ¼ cup fresh basil, chopped
- 1 package crumbled feta cheese
- 1 pint of grape tomatoes, halved
- 1 ½ tbsp fresh lemon juice
- 1 tsp lemon rind, grated
- ¼ tsp pepper
- Fresh basil leaves for garnishing

Directions

1. Heat the broth and seasonings that come in the couscous packet in the microwave on high power for 3 to 5 minutes or until the broth comes to a boil.
2. Put couscous in a bowl and mix in the broth mixture. Allow it to stand for 5 minutes.
3. Fluff couscous with a fork before adding in chicken and other ingredients.
4. Garnish with basil leaves (optional).
5. Serve warm or cold. Enjoy!

Day 4: Devilishly Dark Brownie for the Diet Conscious

Do you want to make brownies?

But don't have an oven?

Or are you worried about packing on those unwanted calories?

Then hop on to the microwavable 'no-bake desserts' train! We have got a recipe for a rich decadent dark brownie. That won't ruin your diet!

Ingredients (Serves 1)

- ¼ cup of whole wheat flour
- A pinch of kosher salt
- ¼ cup brown sugar
- One-eighth tsp baking powder
- 1-2 tbsp cocoa powder
- 2 tbsp of almond milk
- 1 tbsp of margarine
- ½ cup of toasted nuts
- ½ cup of dark chocolate chips

Directions

1. Combine all the dry ingredients (except nuts and chocolate chips) in a medium-sized bowl.
2. Add the milk and margarine. Stir well until the batter is smooth.
3. Use a small microwave-friendly bowl and grease it with some margarine.
4. Then pour the batter in.
5. Now sprinkle in the nuts and chocolate chips.

6. Level the batter in the bowl. Then pop it in the microwave for 5 minutes.
7. Check if it's done by inserting a toothpick or fork in. If the utensil comes out clean then it is done.

Feel free to gobble down this blissful dessert without a guilty conscience!

Day 5: DIY Corn on the Cob

What is not to love about a tender and yummy corn on a hot summer evening? If you are depriving yourself of this simply yet healthy and delicious dish only because you do not have time to prepare it, we have a perfect solution for you.

Here is a simple microwave recipe to give you the delicious corn on the cob that can easily suffice your craving.

Ingredients: (*Serves 2*)

- 2 cobs of corn
- 2 tablespoons of water
- 2 tablespoon of butter

Directions:

- In the microwave, arrange the cobs of corn in a microwave-safe plate.
- Drop two tablespoon of water on the base of the plate with corns before covering them with another plate.
- Microwave for five minutes or until the color of kernels changes. If you want softer corns, you can microwave for an additional minute.
- Drain the water from the plate and spread butter on the cobs.
- Allow to cool and enjoy!

Day 6: Easy DIY Microwave Popcorn

One of the cool ways to spend the weekend night at home is spending time with family with fresh and deliciously home-made popcorn to go round. This snack will take you just five minutes to prepare! Here is a quick simple recipe.

Ingredients: *(Serves 6)*

- 1/3 cup of popcorn
- 2 -3 tablespoon melted butter
- Salt to taste

Directions:

- Pour the kernels in a microwave-safe paper bag (or oven bag). Also, you could use microwave popcorn popper if you have one. The size of the bag can vary on your preference. A standard lunch size is recommended.
- Fold the top of the bag twice. Ensure that every fold is 1/2 inches deep to give room to the kernels to pop.
- Staple the bag to seal it.
- Place the bag in the microwave and cook for 2 to 3 minutes or until the kernels begin to pop.
- Pour the melted butter into the bag.
- Add salt and shake the bag well to distribute evenly.

Day 7: Easy Microwave-Baked Potatoes

Having a steak party at home but have no time for fancy sidelines? Don't worry; we are here to rescue you through with this very simple and super easy recipe of baked potatoes that you can cook in the microwave.

With just a few ingredients and just a few minutes to prepare, you will have your appetizing sideline ready to go with the main course.

Ingredients: (*Serves 1*)

- 1 large potato
- 1 tablespoon butter or margarine
- 3 tablespoons of shredded cheddar cheese
- Salt and pepper to taste
- 3 teaspoons of sour cream

Directions:

- Scrub the potato well and using a fork, prick several times.
- Placing it on a microwave-safe plate, cook on high heat in the microwave for about five minutes. There is no need to cover the plate while potato cooks.
- Turn it over and cook for another five minutes or until the potato is soft.
- Remove and cut the potato into halves lengthwise.
- Season with salt and pepper and mash it using a fork.
- Spread butter on the top and place two tablespoons of cheese.
- Let the potato cook in the microwave again for about a minute until the cheese starts melting.
- Dish it up and garnish using cheese and sour cream.

Day 8: How to Make Extra Flaky Salmon in Microwave?

If you are a seafood lover but you are too lazy to make something because of complicated recipes, this flaky salmon is just the dish for you.

Cooked in merely 10 minutes, this quick and simple recipe will give you a mouthwatering meal.

Ingredients: *(Serves 2)*

- 2 six-ounce Salmon fillets
- 1 tablespoon of olive oil
- 2 cloves of garlic (minced finely)
- 1/4 teaspoon of Kosher salt
- Black ground pepper

Directions:

- In a microwave-safe dish, arrange the salmon fillets. Make sure to keep them skin down.
- Using a brush, spread oil evenly on the fillets and sprinkle minced garlic.
- Season with salt and pepper to taste as per your preference.
- Cover and microwave on high heat for about 1 to 2 minutes or until the fish is done.
- Once the edges are flaky and fish is cooked to the preferred level, switch the oven off.
- Let the fillets sit for a couple of minutes before serving.

Day 9: How to Make 10-Minute Gluten-free Enchiladas in Microwave

Are you looking for a quick recipe to make for a family dinner? These spicy and gluten-free enchiladas are just what you're looking for! In a short time, you can pull out a yummy and healthy meal for your family without going through much trouble. This recipe takes ten minutes to prepare and you are good to go.

Ingredients: *(Serves 4)*

For the Enchiladas

- 3 cups of enchilada sauce
- 12 corn tortillas
- 2 cups of chicken, cooked and diced
- 1 cup of cheese, shredded

For the Enchilada Sauce

- 2 or 3 tablespoons of canola or any other neutral oil
- 3 tablespoons gluten-free rice flour blend
- ¼ cup of red chili powder
- 2 teaspoons of cumin, ground
- 2 teaspoons of garlic powder
- 2 teaspoons of onion powder
- 1 teaspoon of oregano, dried
- Salt to taste
- 1½ cups of chicken broth
- 1½ cups of water

Direction

- In a saucepan mix together all the spices for enchilada sauce with flour and oil. Heat and whisk the ingredients for two to three minutes until they are fragrant.
- As you whisk, add the chicken broth and water and whisk until smooth.
- Heat until the sauce comes to a boil, and then let it simmer for 2-3 minutes.
- Microwave the tortillas for 30 seconds to warm them up. Cover them up with a microwave-safe cover.
- Spread ½ cup of enchilada sauce on a microwave pan.
- In a separate bowl, mix chicken, oregano and one cup of enchilada sauce until they are evenly combined.
- Dip each tortilla in the remaining sauce and spread 2-3 tablespoons of filling. Roll the tortilla and place them in the pan. Repeat the same with the rest of the tortillas.
- Spread the leftover sauce over the enchiladas and sprinkle cheese.
- Microwave for five to seven minutes until the cheese melts. You do not need to cover the enchiladas as they cook.

Day 10: Hot Cup of Mocha Cake

A mug cake is an absolute winner when it comes to satisfying your untimely dessert cravings. Here's an easy recipe for an extra fudgy mug cake that takes under 10 minutes to prepare.

Ingredients: *(Serves 1)*

- 2 tbsp cocoa
- 1 tsp instant coffee granules
- 1 tbsp unsalted butter, softened, and extra for greasing the mug
- 3 tbsp brown sugar
- A pinch of salt
- A pinch of baking soda
- 3 tbsp all-purpose flour
- ¼ tsp maple syrup
- 5 tbsp water
- 2 tbsp bittersweet chocolate chips
- Whipped cream or ice cream to serve on top

Directions

1. Grease the mug with butter.
2. Add the butter, flour, cocoa, brown sugar, coffee, baking soda, salt, maple syrup, water, and chocolate chips to the mug.
3. Stir until mixed well.
4. Cook in the microwave on high power until the cake has risen and looks moist, checking every 30 seconds for about 2 minutes.
5. Do not overcook or else it will be dry.

6. Allow it to cool for a while before topping with whipped cream or ice cream.
7. Chill and serve.

Enjoy!

Day 11: Microwave Breakfast: Quinoa

Do you skip breakfast every morning because you do not have time to fix something fancy to eat? Well, you do not have to do it anymore because we have a yummy quinoa recipe for you! Taking just three minutes to prepare and seven minutes to cook – you will have a delicious and healthy breakfast ready within ten minutes.

Ingredients: *(Serves 2)*

- ½ cup quinoa
- 1 cup cold water
- ½ teaspoon of cinnamon
- 2 teaspoons of butter
- Milk or cream to taste
- Maple syrup to taste
- Banana slices

Directions

- Rinse the quinoa well.
- Drain and stir the quinoa into 1 cup of cold water.
- Add ½ teaspoon of cinnamon and 1 teaspoon of butter into the quinoa mixture.
- Place the quinoa in the microwave, cover and heat for four minutes on high power.
- Stir and heat again for three minutes.
- Remove it from the microwave, cover with foil and let it sit for two minutes,

- Stir in the remaining butter and divide the quinoa into two portions.
- Top with milk, maple syrup, banana slices and cinnamon to taste.

Day 12: Microwave Mug Meal: Pizza

Are you craving for a hot cheesy pizza? But waiting for delivery is too agonizing. And making it yourself is out of the question. So how do you satisfy your hunger?

You do it by making the microwave version of a pizza. This easy pizza mug recipe splendidly serves a super hungry soul!

Ingredients: (Serves 1)

Base:

- ½ cup of all-purpose flour
- sssssss¼ tsp baking powder
- 1/8 tbsp baking soda
- ¼ tsp kosher salt
- 2 tbsp olive oil
- 6 tbsp milk

Topping:

- 4 tsp marinara sauce
- 2 oz of shredded mozzarella cheese
- ½ sliced tomato
- Other veggies (optional)
- ½ tsp of fresh herbs for garnish

Directions:

1. Mix in the dry ingredients for the base in a large microwaveable mug.
2. Add oil and milk. Stir well.

3. Spread your sauce on the base batter and sprinkle it with cheese on. Add the tomato and herbs on top. (You can add other favorite toppings too)

4. Keep in the microwave for approximately 90 seconds or wait until the cheese starts to bubble.

Pro-tip: Don't cover the mug as it will hinder the cooking process.

Now, dig in!

Day 13: Mugged Meatloaf for Quick Meals

Quick meals do not always have to be boring or unfulfilling. With this quick and easy meatloaf in a mug recipe, make your mealtime fun and nutrition-filled. Prepared in just a few minutes, this is a go-to meat recipe enjoyed by both children and adults alike.

Ingredients: *(Serves 1)*

- ¼ lb lean ground beef
- 2 tbsp milk
- 2 tbsp quick cooking oats
- 1 tbsp ketchup, and more for serving
- 1 full tsp dry onion soup mix
- 8-ounce mug

Directions

1. Add the milk, ketchup, oats, and dry onion soup mix to a mixing bowl. Mix well until all ingredients are blended.
2. Crumble and add the ground beef to the mixture.
3. Place the beef mixture in an 8-ounce mug and press firmly.
4. Cook in the microwave for about 3 minutes or until done.
5. Add ketchup or other desired toppings before serving.

Enjoy!

Day 14: October Special: Spiced Pumpkin Cake in a Mug

With winter taking over and cool breezes ready to restrict you to the coziness of your homes, desserts are the ultimate pleasing source to warm you. This spiced pumpkin cake is tremendously easy to make and takes merely a couple of minutes to cook. The best part is that you can cook it in a mug! Follow this recipe and treat yourself with mouthwatering mug cake using just five ingredients.

Ingredients: *(Serves 1)*

- 3 tablespoons of white cake mix
- 1 tablespoon of pumpkin puree
- 1 tablespoon water
- 1/2 teaspoon pumpkin pie spice
- Whipped cream for garnishing

Directions

- In a greased microwave-safe mug, combine white cake mix, pumpkin puree, pumpkin pie spice and water.
- Using a fork, mix the ingredients thoroughly until a smooth mixture is formed.
- Microwave on high power for sixty seconds.
- You can garnish with whipped cream and pumpkin pie spice.

Day 15: Perfectly Easy Poached Eggs

Are you looking to replace your daily deli lunch meals with something healthy and that's easy to prepare? We have the perfect solution for you. This two-minute poached eggs recipe can come really handy. Here is how to make it quick and easily.

Ingredients: *(Serves 1)*

- 1 egg
- 1/3 cup of water
- 1/2 teaspoon vinegar (optional)

Directions:

- Crack the egg into a microwave-safe bowl. You can also use a mug.
- Add 1/3 cup of water into the egg.
- Add vinegar. You can skip adding vinegar if you want to, but it helps the egg coalescing better.
- Cover the bowl or mug with a plate.
- Place it in the microwave and let it cook for 60 seconds. The power of microwave should be retained between 50 and 80%.
- Check the egg and cook for another twenty seconds if it is not done.
- Remove the egg from water and enjoy with salt and pepper seasoning.

Day 16: Potato Soup for the Soul in a Mug

How depressing does it sound that you are depriving yourself of creamy, mouthwatering and delicious potato soup only because it is a lot of hard work to cook? Cheer your taste buds up because we have a perfect solution for your problem. This ten-minute recipe gives you a yummy mug of potato soup to satisfy your cravings. So delve into the details now and get started right away!

Ingredients: *(Serves 1)*

- 2/3 cup of water
- 1/4 cup of potatoes, cut in small cubes
- 1/4 cup of sharp cheddar cheese
- 2 teaspoon of cornstarch
- 1/2 cup of chicken or vegetable stock
- 1/4 cup of milk
- 1/4 teaspoon of garlic powder
- 1/4 teaspoon of onion powder
- Salt and pepper to taste
- Scallions and cheese for topping

Directions:

- In a large mug, add potatoes and water, and microwave it for about 3 minutes. You do not have to cover the mug.
- Once the potatoes cubes are tender enough, drain the water and add milk, stock, seasoning (salt, pepper, garlic and onion powder), and starch to the potatoes in the mug. Stir thoroughly.

- Place the mug back in the microwave and cook for two minutes or until the soup is thick enough.
- Add cheese to the soup and stir until it is melted and mixed well.
- Serve with cheese and scallions on the top.

Day 17: Spicy Microwave Chicken Fajitas

Are you craving for something spicy for a family dinner that is quick and easy to make? Chicken fajitas are the ultimate answer to your taste buds' yearning.

This simple and delicious recipe can help you make a perfect dinner for your family.

Ingredients: *(Serves 6)*

- 2 green or red bell peppers of medium size
- 2 onions of medium size
- 2 cloves of garlic, peeled
- 700 grams of boneless and skinless chicken
- 2 tablespoon of Chipotle Rub
- 12 flour tortillas
- 1 ½ cup of shredded cheese
- 1/2 cup of sour cream
- 1/2 cup of prepared salsa

Directions:

- Slice the bells lengthwise into ¼-inch strips.
- Thinly slice the onions lengthwise and mince the cloves of garlic.
- In a bowl, mix chicken with the vegetables.
- Place the vegetable coated chicken in the microwave and let it cook for twelve to fifteen minutes or until the internal temperature of chicken reaches 165 degrees F. Make sure to cover the dish.

- Cut the chicken into small pieces and stir them back into the vegetables.
- Place the tortillas in the microwave dish for about thirty seconds so that they are warm enough. Cover the tortillas as they warm up.
- Spoon the chicken and vegetable over the tortillas individually and serve immediately with cheese, sour cream and salsa. Salsa seasoning can be replaced with Chipotle Rub.

Day 18: Terrific Time-Saving Tacos

Microwave cooked tacos are the perfect way to make your snack time delicious and effortless.

Here's an easy way to prepare beef tacos in a matter of minutes.

Ingredients: *(Serves 8)*

- 1 pound ground beef

- 1 ½ tsp chili powder

- ½ tsp garlic powder

- $^{1}/_{8}$ tsp cayenne pepper

- ½ tsp salt

- ¼ cup water

- 8 medium taco shells, warmed

- 2 cups shredded lettuce

- 2 cups shredded cheddar cheese

- 1 medium tomato, chopped

- ¼ cup finely chopped onion

- Taco sauce

Directions

1. Crumble the ground beef and place in a casserole dish. Cover with a lid.

2. Cook in the microwave for 5 minutes on high power.

3. Drain and then mix in chili powder, garlic powder, salt, cayenne pepper, and water.

4. Cover with a lid and cook in the microwave for another 3 to 4 minutes on high power or until done.

5. Fill each taco shell with 2 tablespoons of ground beef.

6. On top, add cheese, lettuce, tomato, onion, and taco sauce as much as you desire.

7. Serve with taco sauce.

Enjoy!

Day 19: Three-minute French Toasts

Are you looking for something that is both tasty and fulfilling to power you through until your lunchtime? Here's the ultimate French toast recipe that will be ready in less than five minutes.

Ingredients: *(Serves 1)*

- 3 tbsp whole milk
- 1 tsp butter
- 1 large egg
- 1 cup bread pieces
- 1 tsp maple syrup
- ¼ tsp cinnamon
- A pinch of ground nutmeg

Optional toppings

- Sliced bananas
- Nuts
- Berries
- Powdered sugar
- Chocolate chips
- Peanut butter

Directions

1. Place the butter in a microwave-safe mug and heat for 15 to 20 seconds or until the butter is melted.
2. Add the milk, egg, maple syrup, cinnamon, and nutmeg to the mug and whisk properly until all ingredients are mixed well.

3. Add the bread pieces to the mug and wait until they are saturated with the egg and milk mixture, stirring gently.

4. Wait for about 1 minute, allowing the bread pieces to sit and absorb the liquid.

5. Place the mug in the microwave and cook for about 60 to 90 seconds or until the mixture turns solid.

6. Top with your favorite add-ons and serve immediately.

Enjoy!

Day 20: Very Special Speedy Pancakes

What else can be more appetizing than a fluffy, syrupy pancake in the morning? With this quick and easy recipe, you won't have to miss out on a healthy start to your day anymore!

Ingredients: *(Serves 4)*

- 1 egg
- 1 cup flour
- 1 tsp baking powder
- 1 tsp sugar
- 4 tbsp oil
- 2 tbsp melted butter
- ¾ cup of milk
- Maple syrup for topping

Directions

1. Place all dry ingredients in a bowl and mix.
2. Add all wet ingredients and whisk properly to get a thick consistency.
3. Spread a sheet of greaseproof baking paper on a plate. Place a spoonful of the batter on the paper.
4. Put another sheet of baking paper on top and add another spoonful of the batter on top.
5. Repeat and once you have laid four spoonfuls of the batter, add a final sheet of baking paper on top.
6. Cook in the microwave for 2 to 3 minutes or until done.

7. Separate the pancakes and dress with butter and maple syrup.

Enjoy a quick yet tasty, nutrition-filled breakfast!

Day 21: 5 Minutes Mac and Cheese

Do you love Mac & Cheese?

This traditional dish is the staple of many dorm rooms and student homes. This is because it is super easy to make. The best part is that it requires minimum ingredients with no more than five minutes of cooking time.

Are you ready to give it a try?

Here is what you have to do:

Ingredients: (Serves 1)

- ⅓ cup of macaroni
- ¾ cup cold water
- 4 tbsp of milk
- ¼ tsp of corn flour
- 4 tbsp of grated cheddar cheese
- A pinch of salt
- A pinch of pepper

Directions:

1. Use a large microwave-friendly bowl to boil the macaroni in water. Place the macaroni and pour the water.
2. Pop the bowl in the microwave for approximately 3 minutes or until the macaroni is perfectly cooked.
3. Once done, strain the remaining water.
4. Then add the other ingredients in your macaroni bowl. Mix well.
5. Microwave for one minute.

Enjoy this simple rendition of your favorite go-to meal!

Day 22: Microwave Meals: Scrumptious Chicken Kiev

Do you know what the worst part about making most appetizers is?

It is all the frying one has to do. Don't you wish that we could just speed things up with a less-sweaty option?

Well, your wish is our command. May we present to you the hassle-free version of chicken kiev?

Here is the recipe:

Ingredients: (Serves 4)

- 4 boneless chicken breast (in halves)
- 5 tbsp melted butter
- ¼ tsp white pepper
- ¼ tsp garlic powder
- ½ tsp chives (minced)

For coating

- 5 ½ tsp of cornflake crumbs
- ½ tsp parsley flakes (dried)
- ¼ tsp paprika
- 1 tbsp of shredded parmesan cheese

Directions:

1. Use a small bowl to combine chives, pepper, garlic powder, and 3 tablespoons of butter. Shape the mixture in four equal-sized cubes.
2. Cover your butter cubes and freeze them for 10 minutes.

3. In the meantime, pound the chicken halves until they are ¼ inches thick.

4. Next, place your frozen butter cubes at the center of each chicken breast. Fold the ends over the butter and use a toothpick to secure the folds.

5. Mix cheese, cornflakes crumbs, and other ingredients in a bowl. And put the remaining butter in another bowl.

6. Dip your chicken in the butter then evenly coat it with the crumb mixture.

7. Place the chicken piece in a microwave-friendly dish. (Seam side facing down!)

8. Keep the dish, uncovered, in the microwave for 5-7 minutes. Or until the chicken looks done.

Remember to remove the toothpicks before you bite into this appetizing meal!

Day 23: Microwave Meal: Chicken Quesadilla

Don't have time to make a meal? What do you do?

Order in, of course!

But what about your *diet plan*?

If you find yourself in this dilemma then don't worry. We have a super quick five-minute meal designed especially for those busy lunch hours.

Here is what you need:

Ingredients: (Serves 1)

- 2 tortillas
- 3 oz of sliced deli chicken
- ¼ cup grated cheese
- A pinch of spinach leaves
- ½ a tomato (diced)
- ½ an onion (diced)
- ½ Bell peppers (sliced)

Instructions:

1. Place the tortillas on a microwave-safe plate. Put it in the microwave for 20 seconds or until they are crispy. Take it out to cool.
2. Combine your deli chicken with the veggies in a bowl.
3. Evenly spread the chicken mix on one of the tortillas. Then top it with generous helpings of grated cheese. Cover the tortilla with a second tortilla.

4. Pop it back in the microwave and let it cook for 30-60 seconds.

5. Slice and serve with salsa!

Enjoy!

Don't you wish all your meals got ready this quick?

Day 24: Spot-On Microwave Chili

Do you love spicy food?

Then we bet you would find a hot bowl of freshly stewed chili irresistible.

That is why we came with our very own microwave rendition of this mind-blowing meal.

So that you can get your heat on at super speed!

Here is what you have to do:

Ingredients: (Serves 2)

- 1 lb beef (chopped)
- 16 oz of fresh tomatoes (chopped)
- 1 can of kidney beans
- 1 onion (chopped)
- 3 tbsp of red chili powder
- 1 bell pepper (sliced)
- A dab of butter
- A dash of cumin powder
- 1 tsp of salt
- 1 tsp of black pepper

Directions:

1. First, take a big microwave-friendly bowl and brown your beef. This will take 5-10 minutes depending on your cut. Pierce the beef to check if it's cooked.
2. Once the beef is ready, add all the ingredients. Mix everything well.

3. Cover them with a cling film and puncture it with a few holes. Then microwave them for 7-10 minutes or until done.

Voila! Your chili is ready!

Day 25: No-Bake Chocolate Chip Cookies

Are you looking for something that satisfies your sweet tooth?

Then make way for a simpler version of richly textured chocolate chip cookies. Our mug-sized recipe makes for a yummy snack for all the times you get those sweet cravings.

The best part is that you don't have to bake a big batch or slave over the hot oven. Just pop your mug in a microwave and get that delicious cookie out.

Do you want to know how?

Here is what you need to do:

Ingredients (serves 1):

- ¼ cup of flour
- ¼ tsp of baking powder
- 3 pinches of salt
- ¼ tsp of maple syrup
- 1 tbsp of white sugar
- 1 tbsp of brown sugar
- 2 tbsp of melted butter
- 1 tbsp of chocolate chips

Directions:

1. Take a small microwavable mug and melt your butter in the microwave for 5 seconds. Let the mug cool a bit.

2. Then combine all the other ingredients (except the chocolate chips) in the mug. Mix it thoroughly until the batter become doughy.
3. Fold in the chocolate chips in your cookie dough.
4. Now, place the mug back in the microwave. Heat it for 60-75 seconds or until the mixture forms a cookie-like texture.

Devour your freshly 'baked' cookie with a warm cup of coffee!

Day 26: Microwave Meal: Egg Fried Rice

Don't you just love egg fried rice?

The crunchy texture, the flavorsome veggies, and the soft egg flakes, yummy! What if we told you that you can enjoy all these classic Chinese flavors in a modern mug dish??

Here is what you have to do to experience the single serving splendor:

Ingredients: (Serves 1)

- 1 cup cooked rice
- 2 tbsp red pepper
- ½ sliced stalk of green onions
- Shredded green cabbage (just a pinch!)
- ½ cup of your favorite freshly chopped vegetables

For the egg

- 1 large egg
- 1 tbsp coconut aminos
- ½ tsp sesame oil
- ½ tsp onion powder
- ¼ tsp five-spice powder

Directions:

1. Put your cooked rice in a large microwave-friendly mug. Place your chosen vegetables and the ones in our list in layers on top of the rice.

2. Cover the mug with cling film. Make sure that it is secured and then puncture two holes through the film. This will allow the steam to pass through the cup.

3. Place your mug in the microwave. Let it cook for 75 seconds.

4. In that interval, take a small bowl to beat the egg. Then add the seasonings (coconut aminos, sesame oil, onion powder, and spices.)

5. Take your mug out and pour in the mixture. Stir it well with the rice and veggies.

6. Repeat step 2. This time let your dish stay in the heat for 80-90 seconds or until done.

7. Once done, let the rice cool for a minute.

Then eat up!

Day 27: Gooey Banana Bread in a Mug

Do you know what the characteristics of a perfect banana bread are?
It has to be soft, moist and packed with bananas. You may have known
this already. But did you know that you can make this bread in the
microwave?

Sounds impossible!

Here is the recipe that proves otherwise:

Ingredients: (Serves 1)

Dry ingredients:

- 3 tbsp flour
- 1 tbsp of sugar
- 2 tbsp brown sugar
- A pinch of salt
- One- eighth tsp baking powder
- One-eighth tsp of baking soda

Other ingredients:

- 1 egg or flax egg
- ¼ tsp maple syrup
- 1 tbsp vegetable oil
- 1 tbsp milk
- 1 mashed banana (ripe)

Directions:

1.   Take a small bowl to mix the dry ingredients in.

2. Then combine the dry mixture with the remaining ingredients. Now, whisk until batter turns smooth.

3. Grease a large microwave-friendly mug. Then pour the mixture in.

4. Place the uncovered mug in the microwave. Let it cook for 90 seconds then check if it's done with a toothpick.

5. Keep checking the bread after an interval of 10 seconds until the toothpick comes out clean.

Once done, breathe in the heavenly aroma of freshly made banana bread and devour it!

Day 28: Grill Cheats: Microwave 'Grilled' Cheese Sandwich

What's your favorite comfort food?

We bet a great grilled cheese sandwich is on the list. Are we right?

It is interesting to note that a grilled cheese sandwich doesn't require a grill to be perfect. It can be easily made inside a microwave.

All you want from it is the crunchiness and oozing cheese. Yummy!

Are you ready to make a grilled cheese sandwich?

Here is what you have to do:

Ingredients: (Serves 1)

- 2 Slices of bread
- 2 slices of cheese
- A dab of butter

Directions:

1. Toast your bread for extra crunchiness.

2. Spread butter on one side of each toasted bread.

3. Place your cheese slices between the bread. Make sure that the buttered side is facing outwards.

4. Then wrap your sandwich in a paper towel to avoid getting the bread soggy. Keep your wrapped sandwich in a microwave-friendly plate.

5. Pop it in the microwave for 20-30 seconds or until done.

Voila!

Your super cheesy sandwich is ready!

Day 29: Grilled Potatoes

What is the most versatile vegetable in the farmer's market?

It has to be potatoes. They can be fried, roasted, mashed, and grilled.

Thus, this versatility makes them the perfect side dish for any meal.

Are you in the mood for tasty grilled potatoes? Then might we suggest that you speed the process by popping them in a microwave first?

Here is what you have to do:

Ingredients: (Serving 1)

- 2 potatoes
- A dash of salt
- A dash of black pepper
- 2 tbsp of olive oil

Directions:

1. Peel and then slice the potatoes in wedges.
2. Arrange your wedges in a microwave-safe dish. Keep them in the microwave for 7 minutes or more. Flip the sides after every three minutes.
3. Take them out once they are soft and tender.
4. Now, brush them with olive oil and sprinkle them with salt and pepper.
5. Now, place your cooked potatoes on a preheated grill (medium heat)
6. Grill them for around 10-15 minutes or until done. Flip the wedges from time to time so that they are nicely grilled. Keep grilling until they turn golden brown in color.

Once done, eat it with a delicious sauce. Or pair them up with steak!

Day 30: Fantastic Five-Minute Hummus

Do you love dipping your crackers in hummus?

Ever wondered how it is made? Our recipe for hummus is super simple and speedy. It takes only five minutes to recreate the traditional Mediterranean specialty. The best part is, your homemade batch of hummus can be stored in the refrigerator for some time.

Here is what you have to do:

Ingredients: (Serves 4)

- 15 oz of chickpeas (not drained)
- 3 garlic cloves
- ½ cup of tahini
- 2 tbsp of fresh lemon juice
- 1 tsp of sea salt (or normal salt)
- 1 tsp of lemon juice
- 2 tbsp of olive oil
- Paprika (for seasoning)

Directions:

1. First, combine the chickpeas (un-drained) and the garlic cloves in a microwavable bowl. Let it cook in there for 5 minutes.
2. Add this mixture to the blender and blend it with all the other ingredients.
3. You need to keep processing until the mixture is rich and creamy.
4. Refrigerate for 30 minutes for a thick consistency.
5. Serve it with crackers or pita bread.

Enjoy a flavorsome evening with this clever condiment!

Day 31: Instant Bowl of Tomato Soup

Achoooo!

It looks like sneezing season is upon us. This means that it is the right time to dabble in some soup recipes. But the canned concoctions usually turn out to be too bland to slurp from. Are we right?

That is why you must try cooking up your own version of tomato soup. Better yet, switch things up and make an instant bowl of soothing soup for your chilly bones.

Here is what you have to do:

Ingredients: (Serves 4)

- 2- 3 tomatoes (sliced)
- 1 celery (chopped)
- 1 cup chicken broth
- A pinch of salt
- A pinch of freshly grounded black pepper
- 1 tbsp of maple syrup
- One squeeze of fresh lemon juice
- ¼ cup cream

*Cornstarch for extra thickness

Directions:

1. Make a thick tomato puree by combing all the ingredients in a large microwave-friendly bowl.
2. Add cornstarch to thicken the mixture.
3. Place it in the microwave for approximately 4-5 minutes.

4. Bring it out when the concoction starts to steam.

Blow and slurp on your nutritious bowl of warmth!

Day 32: Instant Cheesy Casserole

What is better than a wholesome bowl of casserole?

It is the kind of casserole that is made instantly without much fuss. You know a dish you can pop in the microwave and it's ready in a matter of minutes. But that doesn't sound very casserole-like to us.

So can this *really* be attainable?

Well, yes it can!

Here is what you have to do:

Ingredients: (Serves 1)

- 2 potatoes (chopped)
- 10 oz can of chicken soup
- Chicken or meat strips
- 8 oz of cheddar cheese (shredded)
- 2 tbsp of sour cream
- Sal and pepper (as per your taste)
- Italian herbs (for garnish)

Directions:

1. Take a medium-sized microwave-friendly bowl and mix all the ingredients (except cheese) together. If you want, you can blend the potatoes too, so they may combine well in the mixture.
2. Sprinkle cheese on top of your casserole mixture.

3. Pop your bowl in the microwave for 5 minutes or until the dish is cooked all the way. You will know when it is done by the light golden color of the cheese.

Looks like casserole *can* be made instantly!

Day 33: Lazy-Cook's Instant Lasagna

Do you love the cheesy goodness of freshly baked lasagna?

But making it is a whole other story since our lazy selves can't put in the effort. Neither does our growling stomach have the patience to wait for it to bake. That is why you won't find lasagna on an average household menu, right?

However, this can change if you compromise on the technique and make way for a microwave!

Here is what we are yapping about:

Ingredients: (Serves 1)

- ½ lasagna sheet (fresh)
- ¼ medium green bell pepper (diced)
- 2 ½ cups spinach (chopped)
- ¼ cup ricotta cheese
- ¼ tsp salt
- 1/8 tsp garlic powder
- 6 tbsp plain tomato sauce
- 75 grams of shredded mozzarella

Directions:

1. Your lasagna sheets should be cut in halves. And each strip should be sliced in half again. Then boil the strips. Once boiled, set them aside.
2. Use a bowl to combine the ricotta cheese with bell pepper, salt, garlic powder, and spinach.

3. Now, take a large microwave-friendly mug and pour two tablespoons of sauce inside.
4. Layer it with one piece of lasagna sheet. And top that sheet with the ricotta mixture.
5. Keep on layering it with sauce and ricotta mixture until you reach the last sheet. Sprinkle it with mozzarella.
6. Microwave the mug, uncovered for 90 seconds. Or until the cheese at the top starts to bubble.

Dig into the deliciousness!

Day 34: Microwave Shepherd's Pie

Craving the taste of a classic shepherd's pie?

But your oven is out of order! Then don't fret and head towards your trusty microwave. Yes, *your microwave.* This mini cooking device can make a delicious shepherd's pie *just* the way you like it.

Don't believe us? Try it out yourself!

Here is what you have to do:

Ingredients: (Serves 6)

- 1 kg minced beef
- 3 large potatoes
- 1 egg
- 1 tbsp of butter
- 1 tbsp of milk
- 6 tbsp of tomato sauce
- 1 tbsp of tamarind paste
- 2 tbsp parsley
- One tomato (chopped)
- One onion (chopped)
- Salt and pepper according to taste

Directions:

1. Firstly, prepare mash potatoes. You do this by peeling and dicing your tomatoes into cubes. Then place them in a microwavable dish. Add 2 tbsp of water and allow the potatoes to cook for 10

minutes or until they become tender. Drain the water and start to mash your potatoes.

2. Next, mix the mashed potatoes with the butter, milk, salt, and pepper.

3. In a separate microwave-friendly bowl, combine your minced beef with chopped onions. Heat this beef mix in the microwave for 8 minutes. Keep stirring the meat after an interval of 2 minutes.

4. Test the meat by seeing if it is done. It should have a nice brown color and no icky texture. Once done, drain the juices.

5. Next, add the tomato sauce, tamarind paste, tomato, and parsley to your beef bowl. Mix well.

6. Place your beef mixture in a rectangular serving dish (10x8 inches). Then spread the mashed potatoes on top of the beef mixture.

7. Lastly, brush the pie with whisked egg.

8. Place the dish in the microwave for 20 minutes or more at medium high. Your pie must have a golden brown crust to indicate that it's done.

9. Allow it to cool for 5-10 minutes before serving.

Devour this hearty warm meal on a cold night!

Day 35: Microwave Veggie Biryani

Do you like biryani but hate the hassle of cooking it?

Then try a microwave version of your favorite South Asian meal. Not only does it taste just good, but it is super easy to make.

Here is what you have to do:

Ingredients: (Serves 2)

- 1 ½ cup boiled basmati rice
- 1 medium onion (chopped)
- ¼ cup potatoes (diced)
- ¼ cup green peas
- ¼ cup tomatoes
- 2-3 green chili (chopped)
- 1 tbsp ginger paste
- 1 tbsp garlic paste
- ½ tsp red chili powder
- ¼ tsp turmeric powder
- 1 tbsp coriander powder
- 1 tsp garam masala powder
- A pinch of salt
- 2 tbsp of vegetable oil

*You may add more vegetables of your choice.

Directions:

1. Boil your basmati rice on the stove.

2. Meanwhile, combine all the vegetables and spices in a large microwave-friendly bowl.

3. Add 2 cups of water in your vegetable mixture. Stir well!

4. Pop your veggie mix in the microwave for 10 minutes.

5. Take a separate microwave-friendly bowl to layer your biryani. But first, grease it with some oil.

6. After greasing the bowl, add ½ of your boiled rice in it. Then layer the dish with the vegetable mix.

7. Repeat step 6 until the bowl is filled. Spray the remaining oil on top.

8. Before popping the bowl back in the microwave, cover it well with a cling film. Remember to puncture 2-3 holes in the film to let the steam out.

9. Let the biryani cook for 5 minutes.

Serve with some yummy raita (yogurt-based dressing)!

Day 36: Minute Meals: Parmesan Chicken

Are you feeling hungry? How does a perfectly cooked parmesan chicken sound?

It probably sounds delicious. Yet, you don't have the money or the cooking skills to splurge on this luxury. Does that mean you forget all about this mouth-watering meal?

Nope.

Here is what you do instead of sulking around:

Ingredients: (Serves 2)

- 2 boneless chicken breast halves (4 oz each)
- 4 tsp of coconut aminos
- ¼ teaspoon garlic powder
- One-eighth tsp of black pepper
- A pinch of salt
- A pinch of white pepper
- ¼ cup shredded Parmesan cheese
- 1 tsp melted butter

Directions:

1. Marinate the chicken breast with coconut aminos, garlic powder, salt, black and white pepper. Keep it in the fridge for 15 minutes.
2. Then place the chicken in a microwave-friendly dish. Sprinkle it with cheese and drizzle the melted butter on top.
3. Cover the dish with a cling film. After securing the film, puncture some holes to let the steam out.

4. Then keep it in the microwave for 4-5 minutes or until the chicken is cooked.

5. Pair your dish with some yummy mashed potatoes.

Bon appétit!

Day 37: Single Serving Chocolate Mousse in a Mug

Did you know?

Chocolate mousse is one of the most indulgent desserts in the world. That is probably why people believe that it is hard to make at home. However, that is pure assumption on your part. Anyone can make a melt-in-the-mouth mousse!

In fact, you can do it with *just* three ingredients!

Don't believe us?

Try this out:

Ingredients: (Serves 1)

- 100 g of 75% dark chocolate
- ¾ cup whipping cream
- 8 big marshmallows

To serve:

- Whipped cream
- Shredded chocolate

Directions:

1. Combine all three ingredients in a microwave-friendly mug. Let it set and then microwave for a minute or until done.
2. Next, whip half a cup of cream (sans sugar) until it forms stiff peaks.
3. Then pour your whipped cream in the mug. Fold well to combine the mouth-watering mixture.

4. Decorate the mug with whip cream and finely shredded chocolate.

We think that this is a great way to spend your cheat day!

Day 38: No-Bake Cheesecake (Microwave Edition)

Do you love a slice of New York Cheesecake? Or maybe you enjoy some of the other delectable fruity renditions?

But trying it at home looks super complicated, doesn't it? We are ready to break all stereotypes by introducing you to an easy no-bake cheesecake. This fun dessert is highly indulging and very easy to make. Here is what you have to do:

Ingredients: (Serves 1)

- 1 tbsp of butter
- 2 sheets graham cracker
- 115 g cream cheese, softened
- 2 tbsp of sugar
- 2 drops maple syrup
- Strawberry or raspberry sauce for garnish

Directions:

- First, melt the butter in a small microwave-friendly bowl.
- Next, grease a separate microwave-friendly bowl with the melted butter.
- Then make the crust by crushing the graham crackers and mixing it with the remaining butter. Try to flatten the crust by pressing it with a spoon.
- In a separate bowl, mix the cream cheese, maple syrup, and sugar. Mix everything and ensure that there are no lumps in the mixture.

- Shift your cheesecake batter in the crusted bowl.
- Pop it in the microwave and let it 'bake' for approximately 4 minutes. (Avoid letting the cheese bubble)
- Once done, let it cool down for a few minutes.
- Next, let it chill in the fridge/freezer for half an hour or more.
- Drizzle it with a berry sauce.

Doesn't that sound like a drool-worthy dessert?

Try it out!

Day 39: Not Your Average Nachos

Planning a movie night in?

Then why not pair your popcorns with a crispy side-kick. Do we mean chips?

No way! Discard that bag of Doritos and grab a plate of your homemade nachos. Not only will this microwave-fresh dish taste delicious, it will also be healthier than the average bag of crisps.

Did we spark your interest?

Here is what you have to do:

Ingredients: (Serves 3-4)

- 1 packet of tortilla chips of your choice
- ½ cup seasoned grounded meat (beef)
- ½ cups of cheddar and mozzarella cheese (shredded)
- 1-2 green onions (sliced)
- 1 fresh jalapeño pepper (sliced)
- 1 cilantro (chopped)
- ½ avocado (optional)
- Salt (for taste)
- Black pepper (for taste)

Directions:

1. Take a well-sized frying pan to cook the beef. Add salt, pepper, and onion to mix in the beef. Keep the meat on medium heat on top of the stove. Stir well and try to break the meat apart into small pieces whilst it cooks. Once thoroughly cooked you need to drain the meat juice.

2. Now for the nachos platter, you need to select a microwave-friendly platter to arrange the tortilla chips on. Then spread the beef, cheese, avocado, cilantro and jalapeño pepper on top of the chips. Make sure to add an extra layer of cheese on top of the whole platter.

3. Microwave the nachos at medium heat until your cheese melts. This will take approximately 60-90 seconds.

Serve with sour cream and salsa!

Day 40: One-Minute Oatmeal

Do you know the name of the most nutritious breakfast on the planet? If you said oatmeal, then you are right. Oatmeal is considered as the healthiest meal around the world due to its high fiber content. That is why boarding schools and elderly homes serve scoopfuls of oatmeal to their residents.

But you can make plain old boring oatmeal a lot of fun by making a microwave version. It is super-fast and flavorsome.

Here is what you need to do:

Ingredients (serves 1):

- 2/3 cup milk
- ¼ cup fast-cooking oats
- ¼ cup raisins
- ¼ cup of your favorite dried fruit
- 2tsp of brown sugar
- A pinch of cinnamon

Directions:

1. Use a big microwave-friendly bowl and combine all your ingredients. Stir the mixture well.
2. Place the bowl in the microwave for one minute or until the oatmeal is boiled.
3. Remove the bowl from the microwave and stir the mixture. Then let it cool for a few minutes.

Serve yourself this wholesome breakfast every day!

Day 41: Fall Special: Pumpkin Pie in a Mug

Making a big pumpkin pie for one is a waste of time and energy.

So then should you miss out on this scrumptious delight? Then dive into our version of a delicious mug-filled pumpkin pie.

Ingredients (Serves 1):

- ¼ cup of pumpkin puree

- 1 tbsp of butter

- 2 tbsp of graham cracker crumbs

- 1 egg or flax egg

- 2 tsp of milk

- 2 tbsp of brown sugar

- 1 tsp of pumpkin pie spice

Directions:

1. Use a small a large microwave-friendly mug to melt butter. Heat it in the microwave for 10-15 seconds.

2. To make the crust, press the graham cracker crumbs to the bottom of the mug.

3. Next, take a small bowl to mix the filling by combining all the remaining ingredients together. Stir well.

4. Now, pour the mixture into your crusted mug. Then heat it in the microwave for 2-3 minutes.

5. Test the pie by inserting in a toothpick. If the toothpick comes out clean, it means the pie is ready. Otherwise, you need to keep it in the microwave for a few more minutes.

Serve and Enjoy!

Day 42: Microwave Edition: Scrambled Eggs

Do you skip breakfast? Is it because you don't have time to make something tasty and healthy for yourself??

Don't fret! We have an easy solution to your problem.

All you need is a microwave and the *right* ingredients. They will help you to kick-start your day with a scrumptious morning meal. That too in just two minutes!

Here is what you have to do:

Ingredients: (Serves 1)

- 2 eggs
- 2 tbsp milk
- Pinch of salt
- Pinch of pepper
- A handful of shredded cheese

Directions:

1. Mix your eggs with milk, salt, and pepper in a medium-sized bowl.
2. Beat till the mixture is smooth.
3. Grease your microwave-friendly bowl. Then pour in your egg mixture.
4. Place the mug in microwave on high heat for approximately 45 seconds.
5. Add the cheese and stir well. Place it in the microwave again for 10-15 more seconds or until done.
6. Remove your scrambled eggs and garnish them with herbs.

Enjoy your cheesy scrambled eggs with some warm toast!

Day 43: Seafood Splendor: Easy-to-Make Prawns

Do you love seafood? How about prawns?

The best thing about shellfish is that it may be a hassle to clean, but it gets cooked in a matter of minutes.

Our seafood splendor recipe gets done in few minutes. And it doesn't compromise on flavor either!

How do we make it?

Here is what you have to do:

Ingredients: (Serves 4)

- ½ kg of raw prawns
- 1 small chili pepper (sliced)
- 2 tbsp of spring onions (chopped)
- 2 tsp of garlic (crushed)
- 1/3 cup of peanut oil
- 1 dash of red chili powder
- Salt and pepper according to your taste

Directions:

1. Firstly, you have to thoroughly peel and devein i.e. remove the veins running across your prawns. But leave the tails intact.
2. Wash your prawns and then place them in a microwave-friendly dish.
3. Add all the other ingredients into the prawn filled dish and mix them well.

4. Then pop it in the microwave for 5 minutes. Following the 2-minute interval rule, take the dish out to stir until everything's cooked.
5. Cooked prawns will look pinkish white with a translucent appearance.
6. Serve it with a complementary sauce or dressing.

Pro-tip: Don't cover the dish when placing it in the microwave!

Enjoy!

Day 44: Super-Fast Spinach Soufflé

Do you love devouring a creamy cheesy soufflé?

Isn't it lovely? It is so warm, rich, and gooey. The only problem is that it takes a super long time to make. And you keep getting hungrier by the minute!

This is why drop that baking dish and opt for a microwave. It will save you a whole lot of time and won't test your patience. To make it healthier we added spinach to our list of ingredients.

Here is what you have to do:

Ingredients: (Serves 1)

- 10 oz of freshly chopped spinach
- 1 egg
- 1 tsp of garlic (crushed)
- 1/3 cup of parmesan cheese (grated)
- 1/3 cup of milk
- 1 teaspoon crushed garlic
- One pinch of salt
- One pinch of black pepper
- Italian herbs for garnish

Directions:

1. Use a medium bowl to combine the egg, milk, cheese, garlic, salt, and pepper together. Whisk the batter until it forms a smooth texture.

2. Now take the spinach and fold it in your soufflé mixture.

3. Transfer your soufflé mix in a microwavable ramekin or mug. Cover it with a plastic wrap to allow the dish to cook well in steam.
4. Place it in the microwave in full heat for approximately 3 minutes.
5. Remove the dish and uncover it to release the steam. Then re-cover the dish and pop it back in the microwave. Let it cook for 3 more minutes or until done.
6. Once done let it cool for a few seconds and garnish with herbs.

Dig In!

Day 45: Mess-Free Microwave Spaghetti Bolognese

Do you love Italian cuisine?

Then you must savor every morsel of a splendid Spaghetti Bolognese served in the restaurants. Now, most saucy pasta dishes are usually pretty messy with all the ingredients that go into it.

But we can minimize your prep and cook time by giving this classic dish a modern twist.

Interested? We bet you are!

Here is what you have to do:

Ingredients: (Serves 4)

For spaghetti:

- 300g spaghetti
- 1 tbsp vegetable oil
- 50ml boiling water

For Bolognese sauce:

- 300g lean beef mince
- 1 onion (chopped)
- 1 garlic (chopped)
- 1 carrot (finely diced)
- 2 tomatoes (chopped)
- 1 tsp of oregano
- 1 tsp of black pepper
- I tsp of salt

Directions:

1. Take a large microwave-friendly bowl and combine the chopped vegetables with your minced meat.

2. Cover the bowl with plastic wrap and puncture a few holes in to let steam out. Then place it in the microwave for three minutes.

3. Take out the bowl, uncover the mixture and stir it again to break any clumps. Place it in the microwave for 3 more minutes.

4. Add oregano, salt, and pepper to the mixture. Then re-cover it to cook for 10-15 minutes. Once done, set it aside to cool.

5. Take a separate microwave-friendly bowl for the spaghetti. Pour boiling water over it and drizzle some oil. Then pop the bowl in the microwave for four to ten minutes. Keep cooking until the spaghetti is al dente (has a bite to it)

6. Once done, strain the remaining water and let your spaghetti cool.

7. Serve it with Bolognese sauce.

Bon appétit

Day 46: Speedy Sweet and Sour Meatballs

Are you racing against the clock?

Then drop the slow and steady cooking and opt for something quick. Our recipe for sweet and sour meatballs is a great addition to your dining table. The best part is that they will be done quicker than your kids start screaming for food.

Here is what you have to do:

Ingredients: (Serves 4)

- 1 pound ground chicken
- ½ cup of breadcrumbs
- ¼ cup water
- ¼ tsp of basil (dried)
- ¼ tsp oregano (dried)
- ¼ tsp parsley (dried)
- 1 tsp of garlic powder
- A pinch of salt
- A pinch of black pepper
- 1 egg
- 28 oz of spaghetti sauce (or tomato sauce)
- ½ cup grated parmesan cheese
- 1 cup shredded mozzarella cheese

Directions:

1. In a large bowl combine the ground chicken, breadcrumbs, basil, oregano, parsley, garlic powder, salt, black pepper and egg.

2. Add water to form a thick mixture. Then shape it into ten to fifteen round meatballs.
3. Now, take a medium-sized microwave-friendly serving dish. And place your meatballs in with some space in between each of them.
4. Lather the meatballs with the sauce and parmesan.
5. Next, cover your dish with microwave-safe plastic wrap. And let the meal cook in the microwave for 10-12 minutes or until done.
6. After that uncover your meatballs and add the mozzarella cheese.
7. Pop dish back in the microwave and cook for 30-60 seconds. Let the cheese melt properly for a yummy oozy effect.

Tell the kids to dig in!

Day 47: Steamy Microwave Veggies

Did you know?

Microwave steamed vegetables are healthier than the traditional steam options you have. How is this possible?

This is because the lower cooking time helps them to retain their nutrients and water content. This makes them super soft and nutritious for you.

Thinking about trying this trick?

Here is what you have to do:

Ingredients: (Serves 1)

- 1-3 Carrot
- 1 Broccoli
- A handful of peas
- 2 Bell peppers
- 3 Asparagus
- Other veggies that you may like

*you can steam (microwave) large quantities of vegetables separately too.

Directions:

1. Wash your vegetables and then let them dry.
2. Cut all your veggies in equal-sized pieces.
3. Use a microwave-friendly bowl to place the chopped vegetables in.
4. Next, pour in some water.

5. Cover your bowl with a cling film. Secure the wrap well, leaving no air gaps.

6. Keep your veggies in the microwave for 120 seconds.

7. Next, check if they have turned tender. Flip and rotate the vegetables between intervals so they are steamed well.

8. Cook again for 3-4 minutes. Then test if the veggies are done by checking it with a fork.

9. When you can easily poke through the vegetables with a fork, it means that they are done.

Now enjoy your healthy snack!

Day 48: Super Speedy Stuffed Peppers

Do you want to make a meal that is packed full of flavor yet is healthy too?

Then look no further than our stuffed pepper recipe. The traditional dish has a microwave version that gets done in no time. It also retains the vegetable nutrients better than your normal stuffed peppers.

Interested?

Here is what you have to do:

Ingredients: (Serving 1)

- 2 large-sized bell peppers
- 1/3 cup of rice (preferably brown)
- ½ a can of kidney beans
- ½ cup of corn kernels (fresh or canned)
- 1 tomato (sliced)
- 2 green onions (sliced)
- ¼ tsp of red pepper flakes (crushed)
- ½ cup of mozzarella cheese
- ½ cup of parmesan cheese

Directions:

1. Slice your bell peppers into two halves. Keep the peppers seeded.
2. Next, arrange your bell peppers in a microwave-friendly baking dish. Cover it with a microwave-safe cling film and poke a few holes to let the steam out. Then pop it in the microwave for 4-5 minutes or until the peppers turn tender.

3. Meanwhile, combine tomato (with juice) and rice in a medium-sized microwave-friendly bowl. Then cover it with a cling film and pop it on the microwave after the peppers are done. Keep the rice bowl in the heat for 5-7 minutes or until rice is cooked.

4. Now, add the red pepper flakes with green onions, corn, and kidney beans in the rice bowl. Stir well. Then heat this mixture in the microwave for approximately 3 minutes.

5. After that is ready, add your stuffing inside the heated peppers. Cover them again and then pop them back in the microwave for 4 more minutes.

6. Lastly, top the peppers with cheese. You may melt the cheesy topping inside the microwave for 2 minutes. Or keep it as it is.

Tada! Your speedy stuffed peppers are ready to go!

Day 49: Super-Sonic Recipe for Tandoori Chicken

Did you know?

Tandoori chicken gets its name from the tandoor. It is a cylindrical clay oven that it is baked in. However, in this day and age, you can't find a tandoor in your average household. Does that mean you give up your plans to make the chicken?

No way! You can actually relish in the spicy taste of a traditional tandoori chicken by using a modern microwave technique.

Here is what you have to do:

Ingredients: (Serves 5-7)

- 1 kg chicken
- 1 cup of yogurt
- 3 tsp vegetable oil
- 3 tsp lemon juice
- 2 tsp of chili powder
- 1 tsp of ginger paste
- 1 tsp of garlic paste
- ½ tsp of garam masala
- 2 tsp of coriander powder
- ¼ tsp of black pepper
- 1 tsp of salt

Directions:

1. Using a knife, make rough knife cuts on the chicken. This is so that you can marinade it thoroughly. Then add yogurt and the rest of

the ingredients in a large bowl. Mix your chicken in the mixture and let it marinade for an hour in the refrigerator.

2. After an hour, take out your chicken. Then arrange the chicken pieces in a single layer in a large serving dish (must be microwaveable). Cover the dish with microwavable-plastic wrap. Then let it cook for 5 minutes.

3. Take the dish out, uncover it and flip the sides. Pop it back in the microwave and let it cook for another 5-7 minutes.

4. Test the chicken with a fork. If the fork easily goes through the chicken's surface then it means that it is cooked. Otherwise, let it stay in the microwave until cooked.

Serve it will lemon wedges for a tantalizing taste!

Day 50: Terrific Three Minute Omelet

Do you wake up groggy each morning? Does this leave you with no time for preparing a big breakfast?

Then alter your routine and pick a smaller easier option. Does an omelet sound good?

Here is what you have to do:

Ingredients: (Serves 1)

- 2 eggs
- ¼ cup of fresh spinach
- A pinch of salt
- A pinch of black pepper
- Shredded cheese (optional)

Directions:

1. Crack the eggs in a small bowl. Mix it with the rest of the ingredients.
2. Pour your omelet mixture in a microwave-friendly mug.
3. Pop the uncovered mug in the microwave for 30 seconds and then stir the mix.
4. Now, keep it in the microwave for 1-2 minutes.
5. Make sure to not let the egg boil inside.

Eat Up!

With egg-cellent ideas like these, we guarantee that you will never skip breakfast again!

Printed in Great Britain
by Amazon

80581092R00058